EMMANUEL JOSEPH

The Everyday Alchemist, Turning Routine into Growth, Calm, and Connection

Copyright © 2025 by Emmanuel Joseph

All rights reserved. No part of this publication may be reproduced, stored or transmitted in any form or by any means, electronic, mechanical, photocopying, recording, scanning, or otherwise without written permission from the publisher. It is illegal to copy this book, post it to a website, or distribute it by any other means without permission.

First edition

*This book was professionally typeset on Reedsy.
Find out more at reedsy.com*

Contents

1	Chapter 1: The Morning Ritual	1
2	Chapter 2: Mindful Moments	3
3	Chapter 3: Embracing Nature	5
4	Chapter 4: The Power of Habit	7
5	Chapter 5: Nourishing the Body	8
6	Chapter 6: The Digital Detox	9
7	Chapter 7: Cultivating Gratitude	11
8	Chapter 8: Finding Flow	13
9	Chapter 9: The Art of Saying No	15
10	Chapter 10: The Joy of Learning	17
11	Chapter 11: Building Strong Relationships	18
12	Chapter 12: The Power of Reflection	19
13	Chapter 13: Simplifying Life	20
14	Chapter 14: The Practice of Patience	21
15	Chapter 15: Finding Inner Peace	22
16	Chapter 16: Embracing Change	23
17	Chapter 17: The Journey Continues	24

1

Chapter 1: The Morning Ritual

Every day begins with the promise of a fresh start, a clean slate waiting to be filled. The way we spend our mornings sets the tone for the rest of the day. It's in these early hours that we have the opportunity to anchor ourselves, to find peace, and to prepare for whatever lies ahead. This chapter explores the magic of morning rituals and how they can be harnessed to foster growth, instill calm, and deepen our connections with ourselves and the world around us.

The first light of dawn heralds the beginning of a new day. For many, the sound of an alarm clock is the harbinger of a rushed and chaotic start. However, by transforming our mornings into a sanctuary of peace and productivity, we can set a positive tone for the entire day. One of the simplest yet most powerful ways to do this is through mindfulness. By dedicating just a few minutes each morning to mindful breathing or meditation, we can center ourselves and cultivate a sense of calm that carries us through the day.

Exercise is another cornerstone of a transformative morning ritual. Engaging in physical activity, whether it's a brisk walk, yoga, or a workout, not only invigorates the body but also awakens the mind. Exercise releases endorphins, the body's natural feel-good hormones, which can elevate our mood and enhance our focus. By making exercise a non-negotiable part of our morning routine, we invest in our physical and mental well-being, setting the stage for a productive and fulfilling day.

Finally, nourishing our bodies with a hearty and balanced breakfast is essential for maintaining energy and focus throughout the day. A meal rich in protein, healthy fats, and complex carbohydrates provides the fuel our bodies need to perform at their best. Whether it's a smoothie bowl, oatmeal, or avocado toast, taking the time to prepare and enjoy a nutritious breakfast can be a grounding and pleasurable experience. It's a small act of self-care that pays dividends in our overall health and vitality.

2

Chapter 2: Mindful Moments

In the whirlwind of our daily lives, it's easy to get swept away by the constant stream of tasks and responsibilities. However, by intentionally carving out moments of mindfulness, we can bring a sense of calm and presence into our routines. This chapter explores practical techniques for integrating mindfulness into everyday activities, helping readers cultivate a deeper connection with the present moment.

One simple yet powerful practice is mindful breathing. Taking a few minutes to focus on our breath can anchor us in the present and reduce stress. By paying attention to the sensation of each inhale and exhale, we can create a pocket of calm amidst the chaos. This practice can be done anytime, anywhere, making it a versatile tool for managing stress and enhancing mental clarity.

Gratitude journaling is another effective way to bring mindfulness into our lives. By regularly reflecting on the things we're grateful for, we can shift our focus from what's lacking to what we have. This practice not only fosters a positive mindset but also deepens our appreciation for the small joys in life. Whether it's jotting down three things we're grateful for each day or keeping a dedicated gratitude journal, this practice can have a profound impact on our overall well-being.

Mindful eating is an opportunity to savor and appreciate the nourishment we receive from our food. By slowing down and paying attention to the flavors, textures, and smells of our meals, we can turn eating into a mindful experience. This practice not only enhances our enjoyment of food but also helps us develop a healthier relationship with eating. By being present during meals, we can listen to our body's hunger and fullness cues, promoting mindful and balanced eating habits.

3

Chapter 3: Embracing Nature

Nature has a unique way of grounding us and providing a sense of peace and renewal. In this chapter, we explore the transformative power of spending time outdoors and connecting with the natural world. Whether it's a walk in the park, gardening, or simply sitting under a tree, these experiences can bring about a profound sense of calm and well-being.

Spending time in nature has been shown to reduce stress and improve mental health. The soothing sounds, fresh air, and natural beauty can provide a much-needed escape from the demands of daily life. Whether it's a leisurely stroll or a more vigorous hike, being outdoors allows us to reconnect with the rhythms of nature and find solace in its simplicity.

Gardening is another way to engage with nature and experience its therapeutic benefits. Tending to plants, nurturing their growth, and witnessing their transformations can be incredibly rewarding. Gardening not only provides a sense of purpose and accomplishment but also offers a hands-on way to connect with the earth and appreciate the cycles of life.

Even if we live in urban environments, we can still find ways to incorporate nature into our lives. Creating a small indoor garden, visiting local parks, or simply opening a window to let in fresh air and sunlight can bring nature's benefits into our homes. By making a conscious effort to connect with nature, we can cultivate a sense of calm and rejuvenation that enhances our overall well-being.

4

Chapter 4: The Power of Habit

Habits are the building blocks of our daily lives, shaping our actions and influencing our outcomes. In this chapter, we explore the mechanics of habit formation and how to harness the power of positive habits for personal growth. By understanding how habits work, we can intentionally cultivate routines that support our goals and well-being.

Habits are formed through a loop of cue, routine, and reward. Understanding this cycle allows us to identify the triggers for our habits and make conscious choices about the routines we establish. By replacing negative habits with positive ones, we can create a foundation for lasting change. Real-life examples and insights from psychology provide practical strategies for building new habits and breaking free from detrimental ones.

Consistency is key when it comes to habit formation. By starting small and gradually building up, we can make new habits more manageable and sustainable. Whether it's committing to a daily walk, dedicating time for reading, or practicing mindfulness, small consistent actions add up over time and lead to significant transformations.

Accountability and support play a crucial role in habit formation. Sharing our goals with others, tracking our progress, and celebrating our successes can keep us motivated and on track. By creating a supportive environment and surrounding ourselves with like-minded individuals, we can reinforce our commitment to positive habits and maintain our momentum.

5

Chapter 5: Nourishing the Body

Our bodies are the vessels that carry us through life, and taking care of them is essential for overall well-being. This chapter emphasizes the importance of nourishing our bodies through a balanced diet and regular exercise. By making conscious choices about what we eat and how we move, we can enhance our physical health and vitality.

A balanced diet provides the nutrients our bodies need to function optimally. This chapter offers practical tips for meal planning, cooking, and making healthy food choices. From incorporating more fruits and vegetables to reducing processed foods, readers learn how to create a diet that supports their health and energy levels.

Regular exercise is another cornerstone of physical well-being. Engaging in physical activity not only strengthens our bodies but also boosts our mood and mental clarity. Whether it's finding a workout routine we enjoy, joining a fitness class, or simply staying active throughout the day, regular movement is essential for maintaining our health and vitality.

The connection between physical health and overall well-being is profound. By taking care of our bodies, we enhance our ability to navigate life's challenges with resilience and energy. This chapter provides practical advice on integrating healthy habits into our daily routines, empowering readers to prioritize their physical health and live more vibrant lives.

6

Chapter 6: The Digital Detox

In our hyperconnected world, screens have become an integral part of our lives. While technology brings many benefits, excessive screen time can have detrimental effects on our well-being. This chapter delves into the importance of digital detoxing and offers practical strategies for reducing screen time and reclaiming our attention.

The impact of excessive screen time on mental and physical health is well-documented. From eye strain and disrupted sleep to increased stress and decreased productivity, the negative effects are far-reaching. This chapter explores the science behind these impacts and underscores the importance of setting boundaries with technology.

Implementing a digital detox doesn't mean completely abandoning technology; rather, it's about finding a healthy balance. Readers are encouraged to set specific times for checking emails and social media, create tech-free zones in their homes, and prioritize offline activities. By being intentional about their screen time, they can regain control over their attention and create space for more meaningful experiences.

Finding offline hobbies and activities is a crucial aspect of a successful digital detox. Whether it's reading a book, pursuing a creative project, spending time with loved ones, or simply enjoying nature, these activities provide a refreshing break from screens. This chapter offers ideas and inspiration for offline pursuits that can enrich our lives and enhance our well-being.

7

Chapter 7: Cultivating Gratitude

G ratitude is a powerful practice that can transform our perception of life and enhance our overall well-being. This chapter explores the science and benefits of gratitude, and provides practical techniques for integrating it into our daily routines. By cultivating an attitude of gratitude, readers can shift their focus from what's lacking to the abundance in their lives.

The practice of gratitude has been shown to improve mental health, increase happiness, and strengthen relationships. This chapter delves into the research behind these benefits, highlighting how gratitude can positively impact our emotional and physical well-being. By regularly reflecting on the things we're grateful for, we can foster a positive mindset and increase our resilience to stress.

Gratitude journaling is a simple yet effective way to cultivate gratitude. By dedicating a few minutes each day to write down three things we're grateful for, we can develop a habit of focusing on the positive aspects of our lives. This practice not only helps us appreciate the small joys but also reinforces a sense of contentment and fulfillment.

Expressing gratitude to others is another powerful way to nurture gratitude. Whether it's writing thank-you notes, verbally expressing appreciation, or performing acts of kindness, acknowledging and appreciating the people in our lives can strengthen our connections and create a ripple effect of positivity. This chapter offers practical tips for expressing gratitude and making it a natural part of our interactions.

8

Chapter 8: Finding Flow

Flow is the state of being fully immersed in an activity, where time seems to stand still and we lose ourselves in the task at hand. This chapter explores the concept of flow and how to identify and engage in activities that promote this optimal state of consciousness. By finding flow, readers can experience a sense of fulfillment and productivity in their daily lives.

The experience of flow is characterized by intense focus, a sense of control, and a merging of action and awareness. This chapter delves into the psychology of flow, explaining how it occurs and its benefits. From increased creativity and problem-solving abilities to greater satisfaction and well-being, the advantages of finding flow are far-reaching.

Identifying activities that promote flow is the first step in cultivating this state. Whether it's a hobby, a professional task, or a physical activity, finding what we enjoy and are passionate about is key. By aligning tasks with our strengths and interests, we can increase the likelihood of entering a flow state. This chapter provides practical guidance on how to discover and engage in flow-inducing activities.

Creating the right environment for flow is also crucial. Minimizing distractions, setting clear goals, and challenging ourselves just enough to stay engaged can enhance our ability to enter and sustain a flow state. By making flow a priority in our daily routines, we can elevate our productivity, creativity, and overall sense of well-being.

9

Chapter 9: The Art of Saying No

In a world filled with constant demands and opportunities, setting boundaries is essential for maintaining balance and well-being. This chapter explores the importance of saying no and offers practical advice on how to set boundaries in both personal and professional contexts. By learning the art of saying no, readers can prioritize their own needs and create space for what truly matters.

The fear of disappointing others often makes it difficult to say no. However, constantly saying yes to others can lead to burnout, stress, and resentment. This chapter addresses the psychological and emotional barriers to setting boundaries and provides strategies for overcoming them. By understanding the value of our time and energy, we can make more intentional choices about how we spend them.

Assertive communication is a key skill in setting boundaries. This chapter offers practical tips on how to communicate our needs and limits clearly and respectfully. Whether it's declining additional work assignments, setting limits with friends and family, or creating personal time for self-care, readers learn how to assertively say no without feeling guilty or anxious.

Prioritizing self-care is an essential aspect of boundary-setting. By recognizing the importance of taking care of ourselves, we can better serve others and fulfill our responsibilities. This chapter encourages readers to make self-care a priority, offering practical advice on creating routines and practices that support their physical, emotional, and mental well-being.

10

Chapter 10: The Joy of Learning

Lifelong learning is a journey that enriches our lives and broadens our horizons. In this chapter, we explore the importance of continuous learning and how to cultivate a love for knowledge. By embracing learning as a lifelong pursuit, readers can experience personal growth, creativity, and fulfillment.

The joy of learning lies in curiosity and exploration. Whether it's picking up a new hobby, reading books, or taking online courses, there are countless ways to expand our knowledge and skills. This chapter provides practical tips for finding and pursuing areas of interest, encouraging readers to step outside their comfort zones and embrace new challenges.

Effective learning strategies can make the process more enjoyable and rewarding. This chapter discusses techniques such as active learning, spaced repetition, and hands-on experiences. By incorporating these strategies into their routines, readers can enhance their learning outcomes and retain information more effectively.

Learning is not just about acquiring knowledge; it's also about applying it in meaningful ways. This chapter encourages readers to integrate their new skills and insights into their daily lives. Whether it's using a new language in conversations, applying cooking techniques in the kitchen, or incorporating mindfulness practices into their routine, the joy of learning is amplified when it becomes a part of our lived experience.

11

Chapter 11: Building Strong Relationships

Human connections are the foundation of a fulfilling life. This chapter explores the elements of healthy relationships and offers practical advice on how to nurture and strengthen them. By prioritizing our relationships, we can create a support network that enhances our well-being and happiness.

Communication is the cornerstone of strong relationships. This chapter delves into the importance of active listening, empathy, and open dialogue. By practicing these skills, readers can improve their interactions with others and build deeper connections. Practical tips for effective communication, including conflict resolution and expressing appreciation, are provided.

Empathy is another key component of healthy relationships. This chapter discusses the role of empathy in understanding and supporting others. By putting ourselves in others' shoes and validating their feelings, we can create a sense of trust and mutual respect. Readers learn how to cultivate empathy in their interactions and create a more compassionate and connected world.

Relationships require effort and intentionality. This chapter emphasizes the importance of making time for loved ones, celebrating milestones, and showing appreciation. By prioritizing our relationships and investing in them, we can create lasting bonds that enrich our lives. Practical advice on nurturing friendships, family connections, and romantic relationships is provided.

12

Chapter 12: The Power of Reflection

Reflection is a powerful tool for personal growth and self-awareness. This chapter explores the practice of reflection and how it can help us gain insights into our experiences, identify patterns, and make informed decisions. By incorporating reflection into our routines, we can cultivate a deeper understanding of ourselves and our lives.

Reflection involves taking the time to pause and consider our thoughts, feelings, and actions. This chapter offers practical techniques for reflective practice, such as journaling, meditation, and self-assessment. By creating dedicated time for reflection, readers can gain clarity and perspective on their experiences and make more intentional choices.

Self-reflection allows us to identify patterns in our behavior and thought processes. This chapter discusses how to recognize and address recurring themes that may be holding us back. By understanding these patterns, we can make conscious changes that support our personal growth and well-being.

Reflection also provides an opportunity to celebrate our achievements and learn from our challenges. This chapter encourages readers to acknowledge their progress and appreciate the lessons learned along the way. By embracing both successes and setbacks as valuable experiences, we can approach life with a growth mindset and a sense of resilience.

13

Chapter 13: Simplifying Life

Simplicity brings clarity and peace. In this chapter, we explore the concept of minimalism and its benefits for our well-being. By simplifying our lives, we can create space for what truly matters and cultivate a sense of calm and focus.

Minimalism is about more than just decluttering physical spaces; it's a mindset that encourages intentional living. This chapter discusses the principles of minimalism and how to apply them to various aspects of life. From reducing material possessions to streamlining daily routines, readers learn how to create a simpler, more intentional lifestyle.

Decluttering is a practical way to start simplifying our lives. This chapter offers step-by-step guidance on how to declutter physical spaces, including tips for organizing and letting go of unnecessary items. By creating a clutter-free environment, we can reduce stress and create a sense of order and tranquility.

Simplifying daily routines can also enhance our well-being. This chapter provides practical advice on how to streamline tasks, prioritize activities, and eliminate distractions. By focusing on what truly matters, we can create more time and energy for the things that bring us joy and fulfillment.

14

Chapter 14: The Practice of Patience

In today's fast-paced world, patience is a virtue that often goes overlooked. This chapter delves into the importance of patience and offers practical techniques for cultivating this essential quality. By learning to be patient, readers can navigate life's challenges with grace and resilience.

Patience is the ability to endure delays and difficulties without becoming frustrated or anxious. This chapter explores the benefits of patience, including reduced stress, improved relationships, and enhanced decision-making. By recognizing the value of patience, readers can approach life's obstacles with a calm and composed mindset.

Cultivating patience involves developing self-awareness and mindfulness. This chapter offers practical exercises for building patience, such as deep breathing, meditation, and progressive relaxation. By practicing these techniques regularly, readers can strengthen their ability to remain patient in various situations.

Patience is also about shifting our perspective on time and expectations. This chapter encourages readers to embrace the present moment and let go of the need for immediate gratification. By focusing on long-term goals and enjoying the process rather than rushing to the outcome, readers can cultivate a sense of contentment and resilience.

15

Chapter 15: Finding Inner Peace

Inner peace is a state of mental and emotional tranquility that allows us to navigate life's ups and downs with grace. This chapter explores practices that promote inner calm and self-compassion, guiding readers on a journey to find tranquility amidst life's chaos.

Meditation is one of the most effective practices for cultivating inner peace. This chapter discusses various meditation techniques, including mindfulness, loving-kindness, and guided meditations. Readers are encouraged to incorporate meditation into their daily routines, using it as a tool to quiet the mind and connect with their inner selves.

Mindfulness is another powerful practice for finding inner peace. By being fully present in the moment, we can reduce stress and increase our awareness of our thoughts and feelings. This chapter offers practical tips for integrating mindfulness into everyday activities, from walking and eating to interacting with others.

Self-compassion is an essential aspect of inner peace. This chapter encourages readers to be kind and gentle with themselves, especially during difficult times. Techniques for practicing self-compassion, such as positive self-talk and self-care rituals, are discussed. By cultivating a compassionate relationship with ourselves, we can create a foundation for lasting inner peace.

16

Chapter 16: Embracing Change

Change is an inevitable part of life, and our ability to navigate it with resilience and adaptability is crucial for personal growth. This chapter explores strategies for embracing change, finding opportunities in challenges, and growing through transitions.

Change often brings uncertainty and discomfort. This chapter discusses the psychological and emotional aspects of change, offering insights into how to manage these feelings. By understanding the nature of change and its impact on our lives, readers can approach transitions with a sense of curiosity and openness.

Resilience is the ability to bounce back from adversity and adapt to new circumstances. This chapter provides practical tips for building resilience, such as maintaining a positive mindset, setting realistic goals, and seeking support from others. By cultivating resilience, readers can navigate change with confidence and strength.

Embracing change also involves finding opportunities for growth and self-discovery. This chapter encourages readers to view change as an invitation to learn and evolve. By stepping outside their comfort zones and embracing new experiences, readers can uncover their potential and create a more fulfilling life.

17

Chapter 17: The Journey Continues

The journey of self-growth is ongoing, and the principles learned in this book can continue to guide readers as they navigate new challenges and opportunities. This concluding chapter encourages readers to apply the insights and practices from the book to various aspects of their lives, fostering continuous transformation.

Reflection on personal growth is essential for identifying progress and setting future intentions. This chapter provides practical advice on how to regularly assess one's journey, celebrate achievements, and set new goals. By making reflection a consistent practice, readers can stay aligned with their values and aspirations.

The principles of growth, calm, and connection can be applied to different areas of life, from career and relationships to personal development and well-being. This chapter encourages readers to explore how these principles can enhance various aspects of their lives, offering practical examples and inspiration.

The journey of self-growth is not a solitary one. This chapter emphasizes the importance of seeking support and sharing experiences with others. Whether it's joining a community, seeking mentorship, or simply connecting with friends and family, readers are encouraged to surround themselves with a supportive network that fosters their growth.

The Everyday Alchemist: Turning Routine into Growth, Calm, and

Connection

In the rush of modern life, we often overlook the magic hidden within our daily routines. **"The Everyday Alchemist"** takes readers on a transformative journey, revealing how simple, intentional practices can turn the ordinary into the extraordinary. Through insightful chapters on mindful moments, the power of habit, embracing nature, and more, this book provides practical techniques for personal growth, inner peace, and stronger connections.

Discover the art of crafting a morning ritual that energizes and grounds you, find pockets of mindfulness in your busy day, and embrace the healing power of nature. Learn to cultivate gratitude, build healthy relationships, and navigate change with resilience. Each chapter is filled with practical advice, reflective exercises, and real-life examples to guide you on your path to a more intentional and fulfilling life.

"The Everyday Alchemist" is a call to awaken the alchemist within you—to see the potential for growth, calm, and connection in every moment. By embracing the magic of routine, you can create a life that is not only productive but also deeply satisfying and meaningful. Whether you're looking to enhance your well-being, deepen your relationships, or simply find more joy in everyday moments, this book is your guide to turning the routine into a masterpiece.

www.ingramcontent.com/pod-product-compliance
Lightning Source LLC
LaVergne TN
LVHW010445070526
838199LV00066B/6205